On the ___8th___ day of ___May___,

in the year of Our Lord ___1982___,

in the Christian Community of ___Our Lady of Fatima___,

located in

___Piscataway N.J.___

___Christopher Jones___

first received Jesus, the Bread of Life,

in Holy Communion.

___Joe + Monica Bahr___

We Celebrate

the Eucharist

We Celebrate the Eucharist

This program also includes Guidelines for Parent and Catechist, Program Director's Manual, and the Celebrations book.

Christiane Brusselmans Brian A. Haggerty

Silver Burdett Company   Morristown, N.J. • Glenview, Ill. • Palo Alto • Dallas • Atlanta

© 1978 Silver Burdett Company

Published simultaneously in Canada.

ISBN 0-382-00012-9

English translation of excerpts from the *Roman Missal*. Copyright © 1973, International Committee on English in the Liturgy, Inc. All rights reserved.

Page 44 — English translation of excerpt from *Eucharistic Prayers for Masses with Children and for Masses of Reconciliation*. Copyright © 1975, International Committee on English in the Liturgy, Inc. All rights reserved.

Photo Credits
The photograph on page 9 left is by Eugene Luttenberg from Editorial Photocolor Archives.

The photograph on page 40 right is by Harald Sund.

All other photographs are from Magnum Photos, Inc. The following are by Burk Uzzle: pages vi, 1, 8 right, 9 right. 16, 17, 24, 25, 32, 33, 41 right, 48, 49 left, 56 left, 57, 64, 65 right.

The remaining Magnum photographs are by Roger Malloch, page 8 left,
Charles Harbutt, page 40 left,
Burt Glinn, page 41 left,
Erich Hartmann, page 49 right,
Marc Riboud, page 56 right,
and Hiroji Kubota, page 65 left.

Katherine R. Wood, at the age of six, did the hand-lettering on the cover and throughout the book.

The art is by Monroe Eisenberg.

Nihil obstat:
Rev. Ronald A. Amandolare *Censor Librorum*
April 19, 1977

Imprimatur:
+ Lawrence B. Casey, D.D. *Bishop of Paterson*
April 25, 1977

The *nihil obstat* and *imprimatur* are official declarations that a book or pamphlet is free of doctrinal and moral error. No implication is contained therein that those who granted the *nihil obstat* and *imprimatur* agree with the contents, opinions, or statements expressed.

Acknowledgments

1. The Eucharist: It's About Belonging. *vi*

2. The Eucharist: It's About Celebrating. *8*

3. The Eucharist: It's About Making Peace. *16*

4. The Eucharist: It's About Listening. *24*

5. The Eucharist: It's About Caring. *32*

6. The Eucharist: It's About Giving Thanks for Creation. *40*

7. The Eucharist: It's About Giving Thanks for New Life. *48*

8. The Eucharist: It's About Sharing a Meal. *56*

9. The Eucharist: It's About Going Forth to Make

     a Better World. *64*

     A Review. *72*

Contents

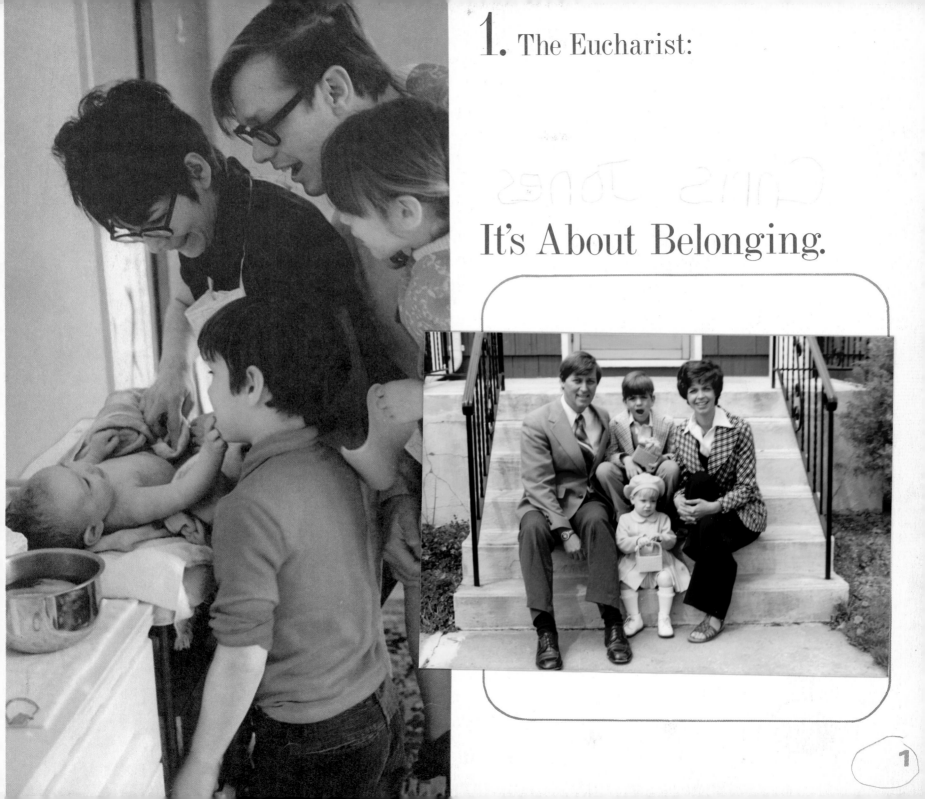

1. The Eucharist:

It's About Belonging.

My name is

Chris Jones

**The name
of my family is**

Jones

**At home, there are
people who love me.**

I love them, too.

Their names are

Joan

Richard

Carrie

2

How good it is to belong to a family.

Here's a drawing of my family and home.

3

When I was a baby,
my mother and father
wanted me to belong
to God's family.

They brought me to
church to be baptized.

The priest welcomed
me into God's house.

He asked my parents,

What name do you give
your child?

They answered,

Christopher Michael

Then the priest asked,
What do you ask of
God's Church for
Christopher ?

My parents answered,
Baptism.

Then the priest asked them,
Will you bring your
child up in the faith?
Will you help your child
love God and neighbor
as Jesus showed us?

My parents answered,
Yes, we will.

Then I was baptized.

Since that day,
I belong to
the family of God!

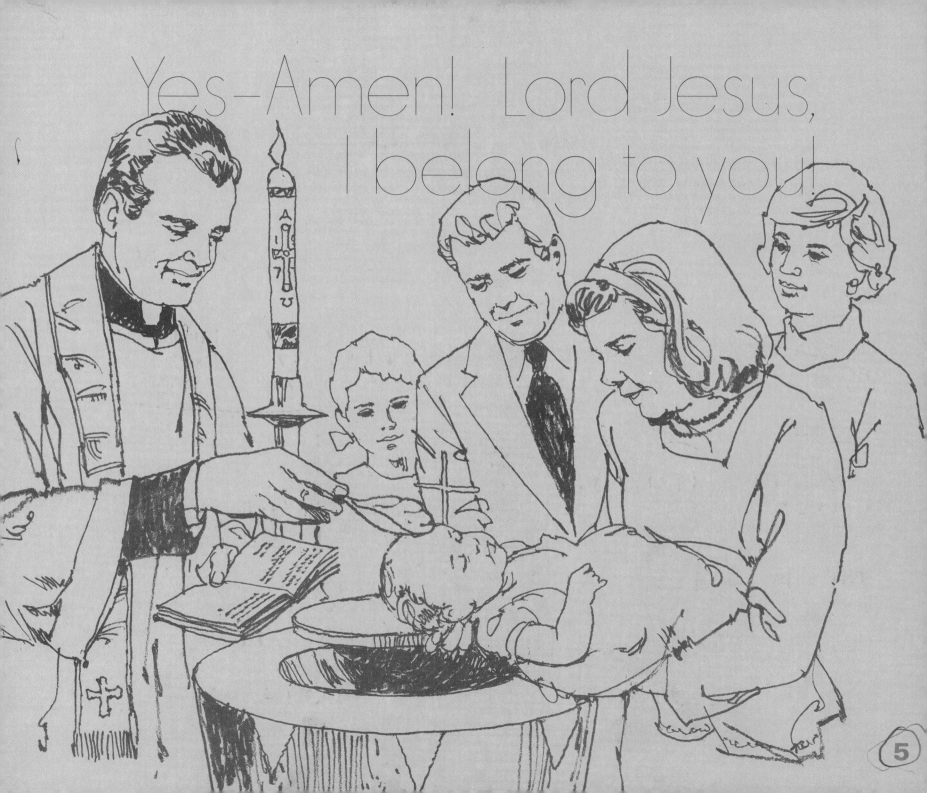

Yes – Amen! Lord Jesus,
I belong to you!

5

God knows me
by my name.
I am his child.
He loves me.

I am very special to God.
I belong to his family.

God says,

I have called you
by your name;
you are mine.

We are God's people.
He loves us!
He has chosen us
for his own.

Most of all,
Let us love one another.
May love make us all one.

Happy are those who belong to God's family.

2. The Eucharist:

It's About Celebrating.

My family loves to have celebrations on special days.

On those days, we invite special people to our home.

On my birthday, I like to invite

Grandma
Grandpa
Michael
Keven
Brian

God gives us a special day every week to celebrate.

It is called

Sunday

On Sunday, my family does many special things.

mass
go out side
visit
trips

Happy are those who love to celebrate life.

This is my drawing of a celebration I liked.

There is a special house
in my neighborhood.

We call it a church.

Many men, women, and
children gather there
to celebrate.

They pray and sing to
the Lord Jesus.

Glory to God in the highest,
and peace to his people
on earth.

Glory to the Lord Jesus,
the son of the Father.

Glory to the Holy Spirit.

Amen.

Jesus says,

Where two or three
are gathered in my name,
there am I in their midst.

Sing joyfully to the Lord, all you lands.

Jesus says,

Come to my celebration;
everything is ready.

Every week Jesus
invites us to a
celebration in church.

We gather with others
in God's family.

We are all Jesus' friends.
We come to celebrate
Jesus, the risen Lord.

Here are the names
of some of the people
who join me in the
celebration.

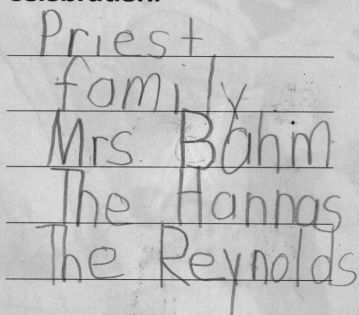

Priest
family
Mrs. Bahm
The Hannas
The Reynolds

Happy are those who celebrate the day of the Lord.

Here I am with my family in God's house.

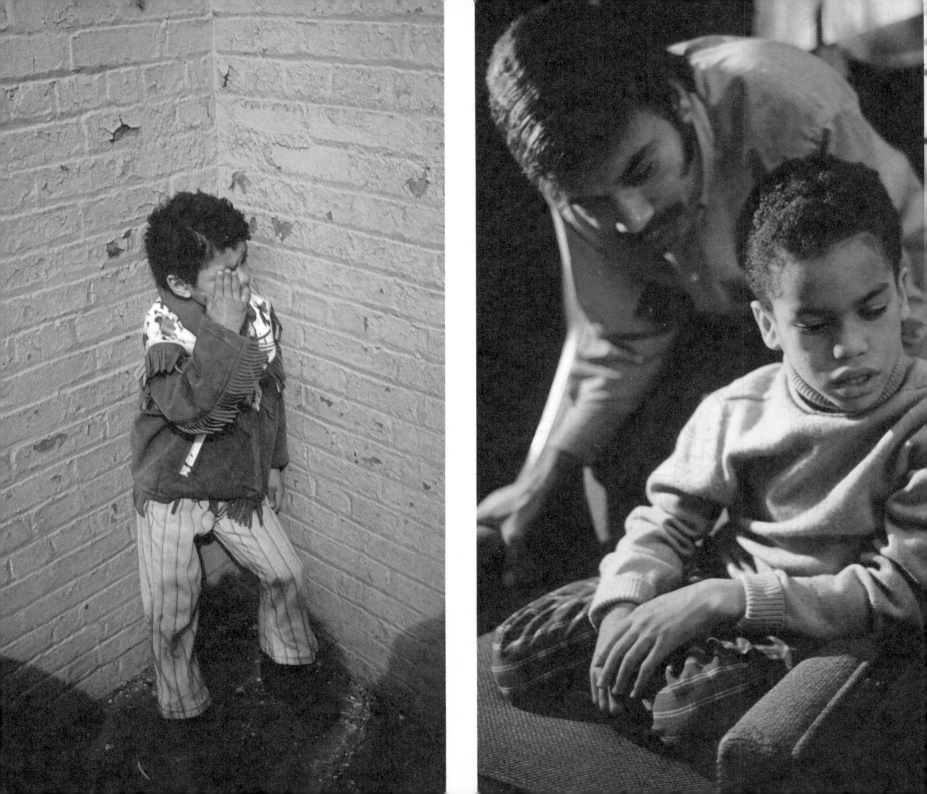

3. The Eucharist:

It's About Making Peace.

17

It is often hard to share,
to play with everybody,
to forgive,
and to make peace.

Sometimes I do not get
along with my parents,
my brothers and sisters.

What can I do about it?

forgive

Don't Yell

Pendence

be Nice

Sometimes I get into
a quarrel at school.

What can I do about it?

tell teacher

I'm sorry

Don't play with

him.

Happy are those who make peace.

Here I am making up after a quarrel.

Jesus says,

My father and I always
forgive those who ask
for forgiveness.

In God's family we ask
for God's forgiveness.

Lord, have mercy.
Christ, have mercy.
Lord, have mercy.

We ask for one another's
forgiveness.

We give one another
the sign of peace.

The peace of the Lord
be with you always.

And also with you.

With Jesus' friend John,
we say,

Lamb of God, you take away
the sins of the world:
have mercy on us.

The
peace
of
Christ
be
with you.

21

The Spirit of Jesus
lives in my heart.

He helps me know how
to please God, and how
to make others happy.

He helps me see when
I have hurt someone.

He helps me to make peace.

Because the Lord has
forgiven you,
forgive one another.

Let your heart
be full of gentleness,
kindness,
and compassion.

May the peace that
Jesus gives
live in your heart.

Happy are those who ask forgiveness
and make peace.

Here are people giving the sign
of peace at mass.

4. The Eucharist:

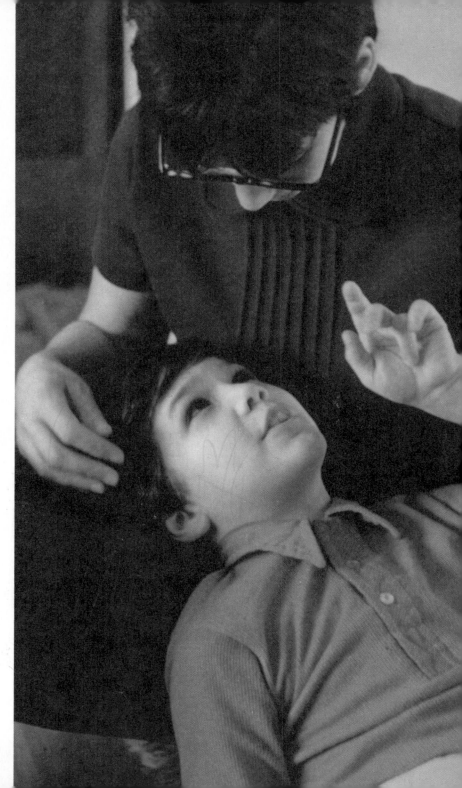

It's About Listening.

There are some sounds
I like to listen to.

There are some voices
I like to hear.

At home, I like to
listen to the sound of

T. V.

On my street, I like to
listen to the sound of

cars

At school, I like to
listen to the sound of

school bell

I also like to listen
to the voices of

Mom
Dad
carrie
teachers

Happy are those who listen well.

Good work

Priest

Gym teacher

bible

Here is someone I like to listen to.

27

At Mass, we listen
carefully to the words
of the prophets and the
apostles.

Their words
are from God.

The readings are taken
from the Bible.

We often sing a psalm
to welcome God's word
into our hearts.

Alleluia, Alleluia!
Your words, O Lord,
are the joy of our hearts.

Jesus says,

I am the word of God.
If you listen to my word,
and do my word,
you are my friends.

We stand and welcome
the Lord Jesus
who speaks to us
through the Holy Gospel.

Praise to you, Lord Jesus Christ.

29

Jesus says,

Happy are those who listen to the word of God and do what it says.

Because we are friends of Jesus, we love to listen to his words.

We can find what Jesus says and does in a book called the Bible.

I remember some of Jesus' words.

Here they are.

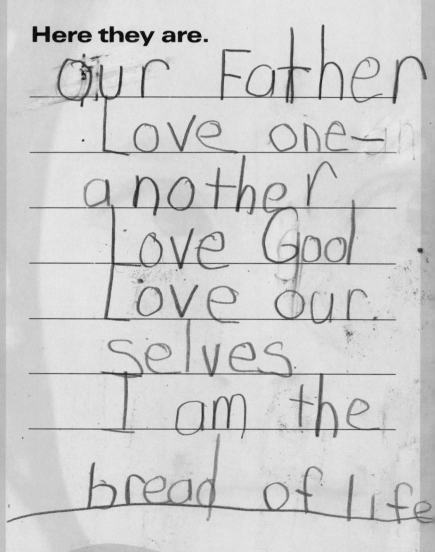

Our Father
Love one-an
another
Love God
Love our
selves
I am the
bread of life

Happy are those who listen to God's Word.

very nice work

dad chris

mom

priest

This is God's family listening to His word.

signature

31

5. The Eucharist:

It's About Caring.

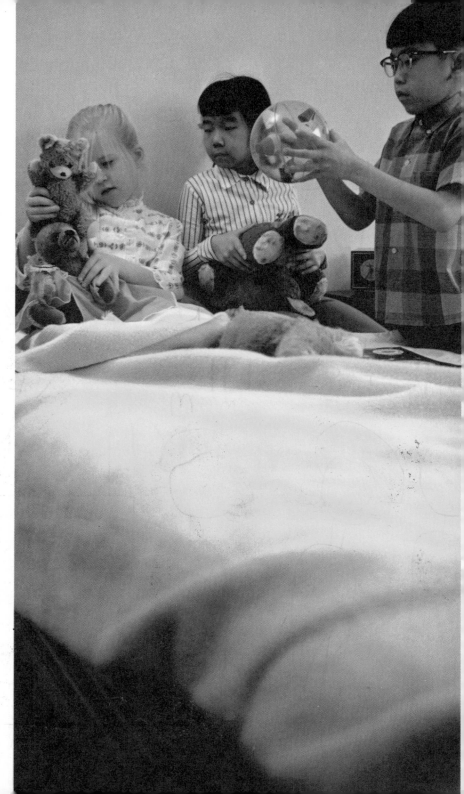

Many people care for me at home, at school, and in my neighborhood. I can care for people, too.

Are there some people I can help?

Someone whom no one ever plays with?

Someone sad or lonely I could talk to?

Is there someone sick whom I could visit?

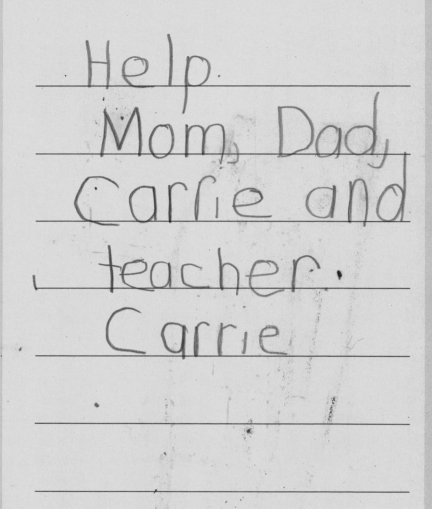

Help.
Mom, Dad,
Carrie and
teacher.
Carrie

Happy are those who care for people.

nice work

Here are some people who need love and care.

With God's family, we pray for one another.

We pray for people who need our special care and love.

The Prayer for the Human Family

For the human family all over the world,

For those who have no home,
For those who have no food,
For those who are sick,
For those who are old or alone,

For those who have no schools,

For those who have no work,
For those who suffer from war,

For our parents and our teachers,

For leaders of our country,
For the leaders of God's family,

Lord, have mercy.

Lord, have mercy.

Jesus says,

Happy are those who make peace.

Happy are those who share with others.

Happy are those who comfort others.

Do I know of people who care for others, and who try to put Jesus' words into practice?

Here are their names.

Priest
President
Fish
Parents
Doctors

Happy are those who open their hearts
to people in need.

Very Good.

for __Mom__

for __Dad__

for __Carrie__

for __Grandmoms__

for __GrandPop__

These **are** people I want to pray for.

39

6. The Eucharist:

It's About Giving Thanks for Creation.

The Prayer of Saint Francis

Praise to you, Lord,
for all creatures!
For our brother the sun,
beautiful and radiant.
By him you give us light.

Praise to you, Lord,
for our brother the wind,
for the air,
and the clouds,
for the clear sky,
and for every kind of
weather.

Praise to you, Lord,
for our sister the water.

She is so useful,
so precious and so pure.

Praise to you, Lord,
for our brother the fire.
He is handsome,
joyous, and strong.
By him you make us warm;
by him you light up
the night.

Praise to you, Lord,
for our mother the earth.
She carries us
and feeds us.
She gives us her plants
and her colorful fruits.

All creatures,
bless the Lord!

Happy are those who give thanks for creation.

Nice wak

dad

mom

Here are some of God's gifts to me.

At Mass we pray:

God our Father,
you have brought us here
    together
so that we can give you thanks
    and praise
for all the wonderful things
    you have done.

We thank you for all that is
    beautiful in the world
and for the happiness you have
    given us.
We praise you for daylight
and for your word which lights
    up our minds.
We praise you for the earth,
and all the people who live on it,
and for our life which comes
    from you.

We know that you are good.
You love us and do great things
    for us.
So we all sing together:

Holy, holy, holy Lord,
    God of power and might,

Heaven and earth are full
    of your glory.

    Hosanna in the highest.

Blessed is he who comes
    in the name of the Lord.

    Hosanna in the highest.

God loves us so much
that he sent Jesus
to save us.

If we open our hearts
to his light and his love,
Jesus will give us
a new life.

He makes us children
of God.

This is my prayer
to thank the Father for
sending us his Son, Jesus.

God.

Thank you
God for
Giving Jesus
you are so
good.

Happy are those who give thanks to the Lord.

God
loves us
so much
that he gives us
his only Son,
Jesus!

Here is how I decorate this page.

47

7. The Eucharist:

It's About Giving Thanks for New Life.

My parents love me more than anyone else does.

They spend their lives and time for me.

This is what my mother does for me:

Helpes me with my home
Make food

This is what my father does for me:

fixs my club house
Gets me toys

I, too, can share my love and life with others.

This is what I can do:

Play in the snow
forGive

Happy are those who share their life and love.

Said

Dater   Police   ARMY

Here are people who share their life
and love with others.

Jesus came to us
to give us his life.
Here is what he did
to stay with us.

At supper, surrounded
by twelve of his best friends,
Jesus took a piece of bread.
He gave thanks.
Then he broke the bread,
gave it to his friends,
and said,

Take this, all of you, and eat it.
This is my body,
which is going to be given
for you.

Do this in memory of me.

Then Jesus took a cup
of wine.
Again he gave thanks.
Then he gave the cup
to his friends,
and said,

Drink from this,
all of you.
This is my life,
which I am giving up
for all of you,
so that your sins
will be forgiven.

Do this in memory of me.

Love one another as I love you!

53

Jesus says,

There is no greater love
than to give your life
for your friends.

Jesus gives his life
for us.
This is what his
sacrifice is.

The Bible says,

Give your life
for one another.
Do not forget
to do good around you.
Share what you have.
These are the sacrifices
God desires.
This is the sacrifice
of Jesus' friends.

Jesus says,

I give you my Spirit.
He will help you
understand all this
and do it.

When we eat this bread and drink
this cup,
we proclaim your death, Lord Jesus,
until you come in glory.

Happy are those who share in the life of Jesus.

gerd

signature

Here is how Jesus shared his life and love with us.

55

8. The Eucharist:

It's About Sharing a Meal.

When we share a meal
with others, we share our
life and love with them.

My parents work
many hours
to buy the food we need.

They share their time and talent
to prepare the food
for the table.

When everything is ready,
we sit at the table and
enjoy our meal together.

We thank God
for the food.

We thank him for the joy
and the love we share.

How can I bring joy
to the meals I share
with my family?

Don't conplane
Get your drink
eat all your food
drink your milk

Happy are those who share a meal.

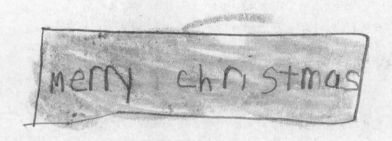

Here's my family eating a special meal.

**The Lord invites us
to share in his meal.**

**The celebrant invites us
in the name of the Lord.**

Happy are those who are
    called to his supper.

**When we see
the Bread of Life,
we say to the Lord,**

Lord, I am not worthy to receive you,
but only say the word and I shall
be healed.

**We go up to receive the
Bread of Life with many
of Jesus' friends.**

The celebrant says,
The Body of Christ.

We answer,
Amen.

**We sing joyfully as we go
to the table of the Lord.**

I receive the risen Lord, and my heart is full of joy.

I am now ready to share
in the meal of the Lord.

Soon I shall make my
first Holy Communion.

When I receive
Communion, I am
one with the Lord,
one with my family,
one with God's family.

The bread I shall receive
is a very special bread.
It is the Bread of Life.

Jesus says,

I am the Bread of Life.
If you eat this bread,
I will live in you
and you in me.

This is my prayer to tell
the Lord how much
I wish to receive him.

Thank You Lord
for being so
good And askin
me to go
to your meal

Happy are those who share in the Lord's meal.

This is how my family and I will celebrate my first Holy Communion.

9. The Eucharist:

It's About Going Forth to Make a Better World.

There are many things we would like others to do for us.

What do my parents, brothers, and sisters do for me?

They Love me

What do my teachers and classmates do for me?

teach me things

What do my neighbors and friends do for me?

Play with me

Happy are those who bring joy and love to others.

This is how I can show my love for others.

After we have received
Communion, we all come
back to our seats.

We keep silent for a
moment.

The Spirit of Jesus
helps us find good ideas
for bringing joy and love
to people.

Jesus says,

My Father
sent me into the world.
Now I send you
into the world!

The celebrant blesses us.

May almighty God bless you,
the Father, and the Son,
and the Holy Spirit.

We make the sign of
the cross and answer,

Amen.

The celebrant sends
us forth.

Go in peace to love
and serve the Lord.

We answer,

Thanks be to God.

We leave God's house
with a joyful song.

Go in peace
to love
and serve
the Lord.

Jesus says to those
who love others
and care for them:

Come and enter into the
kingdom of heaven.

For when I was hungry,
you fed me;

when I was thirsty,
you gave me drink;

when I was a stranger,
you took me home;

when I was naked,
you clothed me;

when I was sick,
you took care of me;

when I was in prison,
you visited me.

Anything you do for any
of my brothers or sisters,
you do for me.

The Lord will come back
one day.

On that day
there will be
no more tears,
no more cries,
no more wars,
no more death.

On that day there will be
no more unhappy people.
God will reward each person
for the good
he or she has done
on this earth.

The Lord says,

I shall make a new heaven
and a new earth.

Blessed are those
who shall enter into
my holy city!

Blessed are those
who shall be invited
to my feast.

In my house I shall gather
every kind of people
from all over the world,
however great or small.

On that day
I shall be with you
forever!

A REVIEW of What I Have Learned to Help Me Grow in God's Family

1. Since when have I belonged to God's family?

I have belonged to God's family since the day I was baptized. On that day, I became a child of God and received my name.

2. When we come together as God's family, is Jesus present among us?

Yes. Jesus says, "Where two or three come together in my name, I am there with them."

3. Why do we go to church on Sunday?

We go to church on Sunday to celebrate the resurrection of Jesus.

4. Why is Sunday called the Lord's Day?

Sunday is called the Lord's Day because it is the day on which Jesus was raised to new life by his Father.

5. Why do we stand and sing at the entrance procession?

We stand and sing at the entrance procession because the celebrant comes among us in the name of Jesus.

6. Who reconciles us with God our Father?

Jesus reconciles us with God our Father and asks us to make peace with one another as well.

7. Of whom do we ask forgiveness in God's family?

In God's family, we ask forgiveness of God and of one another—especially when we pray the Lord's Prayer and offer one another the sign of peace.

8. Why do we stand and sing a gospel acclamation?

We stand and sing a gospel acclamation to welcome Jesus, the Word of God. Jesus is present to us when we listen to his words and live by them.

9. In whose care am I?

I am in the care of God and of those who love me.

10. Whom can I love and care for?

I can love and care for my parents, my sisters and brothers, my friends and teachers, and many other people who need me.

11. What do we give thanks for during the Eucharist?

During the Eucharist, we give thanks to God our Father for the gift of life, for the gift of his Son, Jesus, and for the gift of the Holy Spirit, who lives in our hearts.

12. Why is the Eucharist also called the Holy Sacrifice?

The Eucharist is also called the Holy Sacrifice because it recalls Jesus' gift of his life for the forgiveness of our sins, Jesus' resurrection, and his gift of the Spirit of love.

13. How can we join in the sacrifice of Jesus?

We can join in the sacrifice of Jesus by sharing our love and our life with one another as Jesus did. In this way, we become followers of Jesus.

14. Why is the Eucharist also called the Lord's Supper?

The Eucharist is also called the Lord's Supper because Jesus celebrated the first Eucharist at a special meal that he shared with his friends.

15. Is Jesus present to us when we receive Holy Communion?

Yes. Jesus says, "I am the bread of life. Those who eat this bread live in me and I live in them. Whoever eats this bread will live forever."

16. Why is the Eucharist also called the Mass?

The Eucharist is also called the Mass because the word Mass means "mission." Jesus sends us into the world to carry on his mission of bringing love and peace to everyone.

17. What will Jesus do when he comes in glory?

When Jesus comes in glory, he will gather the human family from all over the world and unite them into God's famiy.

5 6 7 8 9 10—U—84 83 82 81 80